AMERICANS DIVIDED

The Civil War 1860-1865

TITLE LIST

AMERICA DIVIDED: *The Civil War 1860-1865*

BY
SHEILA NELSON

MASON CREST PUBLISHERS
PHILADELPHIA

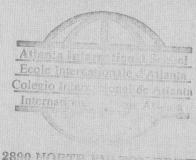

Mason Crest Publishers Inc.
370 Reed Road
Broomall, Pennsylvania 19008
(866) MCP-BOOK (toll free)

First printing
1 2 3 4 5 6 7 8 9 10

Library of Congress Cataloging-in-Publication Data

Nelson, Sheila.
  Americans divided : the Civil War / by Sheila Nelson.
    p. cm. — (How America became America)
  Includes bibliographical references (p.) and index.
  ISBN 1-59084-908-6   ISBN 1-59084-900-0 (series)
  1. United States—History—Civil War, 1861–1865—Juvenile literature.
  2. Reconstruction—Juvenile literature. I. Title. II. Series.
  E468.N423 2005
  973.7—dc22
                          2004011147

Design by Dianne Hodack.
Produced by Harding House Publishing Service, Inc.
Cover design by Dianne Hodack.
Printed in the Hashemite Kingdom of Jordan.

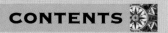

CONTENTS

INTRODUCTION

by Dr. Jack Rakove

Today's America is not the same geographical shape as the first American colonies—and the concept of America has evolved as well over the years.

When the thirteen original states declared their independence from Great Britain, most Americans still lived within one or two hours modern driving time from the Atlantic coast. In other words, the Continental Congress that approved the Declaration of Independence on July 4, 1776, was continental in name only. Yet American leaders like George Washington, Benjamin Franklin, and Thomas Jefferson also believed that the new nation did have a continental destiny. They expected it to stretch at least as far west as the Mississippi River, and they imagined that it could extend even further. The framers of the Federal Constitution of 1787 provided that western territories would join the Union on equal terms with the original states. In 1803, President Jefferson brought that continental vision closer to reality by purchasing the vast Louisiana Territory from France. In the 1840s, negotiations with Britain and a war with Mexico brought the United States to the Pacific Ocean.

This expansion created great opportunities, but it also brought serious costs. As Americans surged westward, they created a new economy of family farms and large plantations. But between the Ohio River and the Gulf of Mexico, expansion also brought the continued growth of plantation slavery for millions of African Americans. Political struggle over the extension of slavery west of the Mississippi was one of the major causes of the Civil War that killed hundreds of thousands of Americans in the 1860s but ended with the destruction of slavery. Creating opportunities for American farmers also meant displacing Native Americans from the lands their ancestors had occupied for centuries. The opening of the west encouraged massive immigration not only from Europe but also from Asia, as Chinese workers came to labor in the California Gold Rush and the building of the railroads.

By the end of the nineteenth century, Americans knew that their great age of territorial expansion was over. But immigration and the growth of modern industrial cities continued to change the American landscape. Now Americans moved back and forth across the continent in search of economic opportunities. African Americans left the South in massive numbers and settled in dense concentrations in the cities of the North. The United States remained a magnet for immigration, but new immigrants came increasingly from Mexico, Central America, and Asia.

Ever since the seventeenth century, expansion and migration across this vast landscape have shaped American history. These books are designed to explain how this process has worked. They tell the story of how modern America became the nation it is today.

Thomas Jefferson

One
THE INSTITUTION OF SLAVERY

The sun beats down on a huge white-columned house. Hundreds of black slaves, stripped to the waist and sweating in the heat, toil in miles of cotton fields. Their mournful songs rise in the humid air. The white overseer rides his horse slowly around the fields, occasionally cracking his whip at a slave moving too slowly.

Is this what you think of when you hear the word slavery? The sprawling plantation with numerous slaves is a common stereotype people have about the pre–Civil War South. Plantations like these did exist, but much more common were smaller farms, worked by fewer slaves. Even most of the larger plantations had fewer than a hundred slaves. Nearly a third of families in the slave states owned slaves, with most of these families owning one or two slaves.

Slavery was introduced in America not long after colonists from England had begun to settle along the coastline. In 1619, a Dutch ship traded twenty Africans to the Jamestown colonists in Virginia. These first Africans were considered indentured servants. This meant that they could earn their freedom after working for a certain number of years. Over the next century, however, slave laws were gradually introduced, until the freedoms of the African workers in America had been completely taken away.

In the beginning, the American colonists en-

Store Room

Store Room

The interior of a slave ship. Human beings were packed in like sardines.

slaved the black Africans for **economic** reasons. The colonists needed workers for their tobacco and rice plantations and slaves were—at that time—cheap. They *rationalized* their actions by saying that black people were inferior and that the slaves were better off in civilized America than they had been in Africa.

Not long after the American Revolution the Southern states started having financial problems. Tobacco crops drained the nutrients from the soil, and tobacco planters were forced to move further and further west to find new land for their crops. The market in England for American tobacco had also dropped off. The slave population increased as children were born to the Africans, and American slave own-ers found themselves with more slaves than they were able to use or sell. It was expensive to care for so many slaves when the economy was so bad. Some slave owners started thinking about setting their slaves free.

Then, in 1793, Eli Whitney invented the cot-ton gin. The cotton gin was a machine that sep-arated the cottonseed from the fibers. Before it was invented, this process had to be done by hand, which was extremely time consuming. It had never been profitable to grow cotton be-cause of the amount of time and effort it took to separate the fibers and get them ready to sell—but the invention of the cotton gin changed all that. Suddenly, everybody wanted to grow cot-ton. Slaves were in demand again, and most

These slave quarters on a Southern plantation are still standing today

Economic *means having to do with money and financial issues.*

*To **rationalize** means to make an action or belief seem reasonable, even though it may not be.*

Aristocrats *are people of the upper class.*

Eli Whitney

slave owners abandoned any idea of freeing them. Even the free states in the North were involved, providing shipping to transport the cotton to England and banks to lend money to finance land purchases on which to grow more cotton.

Some people got very rich growing cotton. Although less than two thousand families owned more than one hundred slaves each, these slave owners lived an extravagantly wealthy lifestyle. These were the slave owners from whom we get the stereotypes of the huge plantations and the many slaves. The wealthiest families were ***aristocrats***. They were the ones who ran the governments. They sent their children to the best private schools and thought of themselves as lords ruling over their own little kingdoms. They

Cotton plant

Scars left on an African American after he was whipped by his white "owners"

even organized tournaments and jousts like medieval knights.

The poorest white people were sometimes nearly as bad off as the slaves. Most of these poor whites defended slavery just as strongly as those who owned dozens of slaves. This might have been because they hoped that one day they would get rich, and then they would be the ones living in huge houses and owning lots of slaves. Or maybe it was because they just felt better

12

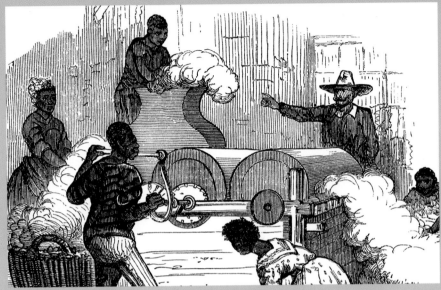

Cotton gin

about their position when they knew they were still better off so-cially than the slaves. Many white people did not realize that black-skinned people were just as valuable, just as human, as they were.

Sometimes slaves were freed as a reward for good service. Unfortunately, some slave owners freed slaves only when the slaves were too old, or ill, or badly injured to work or to sell. The slave owners did not want to care for unprofitable slaves, but the former slaves were then faced with the problem of trying to care for themselves.

Another problem faced by freed slaves was ***racism***. In America at that time, no white people were slaves, but almost all black peo-

Slave auction hall in Atlanta, Georgia

*An **export** is a product or crop that is shipped out of a country in exchange for money or other products.*

*

*Morality** has to do with what is right and wrong.*

*

*Atrocities** are acts of unusual or illegal cruelty.*

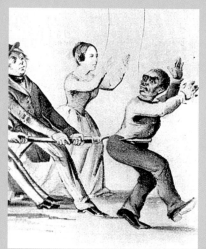

A poster depicting slavery

ple were slaves. Therefore, when someone saw a freeman's black skin they usually immediately assumed he was a slave. Some free blacks were actually captured and sold back into slavery because someone thought (or claimed to think) that they were runaway slaves.

The popularity of cotton as an ***export*** only strengthened the hold of slavery in America. As people continued to grow huge quantities of cotton, the land again began to suffer, just as it had with the tobacco crops. The overfarming by the plantation owners depleted the topsoil until most of it washed away in rainstorms or blew away in the wind. There was still a high demand for cotton overseas, though, so the western territories started to look very attractive to cotton growers.

When the Southern slave states began looking toward the west, some people in the Northern free states started to get nervous about the expansion of slavery. They had two main reasons for their anxiety.

First of all, they were worried about the ***morality*** of slavery. The abolitionists who wanted to outlaw slavery believed that it was wrong to enslave other human beings. They read the slave narratives written by escaped slaves and books like *Uncle Tom's Cabin*, by Harriet Beecher Stowe, and they were horrified at the conditions slaves had to endure.

Some cite the publication of *Uncle Tom's Cabin; or, Life Among the Lowly* as a cause of the Civil War. Although that might not be the complete truth, the work by Harriet Beecher Stowe did awaken many to the ***atrocities*** of slavery.

The second reason for Northern anxiety was that some people thought slaves were doing jobs poor white people could be paid to do. For a while, the American Colonization Society worked to take freed slaves back to Africa. In 1822, the Republic of Liberia was founded with former slaves. As far as the white Northerners were concerned, this satisfied both of the problems with slavery. Many African Americans did not want to go to Africa, however. They had been born into slavery in America and this was the only home they knew. The colonization effort was short-lived.

With the slave owners in the South thinking about taking slavery west with them and the Northerners worrying about how to stop the spread of slavery, America was beginning to split into two separate parts. Slavery had become a dividing issue.

15

A cotton plant

Harriet Beecher Stowe

Harriet Beecher was born in Litchfield, Connecticut, on June 14, 1811. She was the seventh of eleven children born to Roxana and Lyman Beecher. Roxana Beecher was an early proponent of educational opportunities for women. Her daughter Catherine was an innovator in women's education, and Harriet was given the benefits of a fine education. Her father, Lyman, was a Congregationalist minister and an outspoken supporter of the abolitionist movement. Harriet's brother Henry Ward Beecher was also a minister and became a leader of the abolitionist movement.

In 1836, Harriet married Calvin Stowe. While living in Cincinnati, Ohio, and raising her family, Harriet became personally aware of the sadness of slavery. She and Calvin discovered that their servant, Zillah, was a runaway slave. Calvin and Harriet's brother Henry took Zillah to the next stop on the Underground Railroad so she would be further away from the slave states.

The passage of the Fugitive Slave Act, making it illegal to help runaway slaves, inspired Harriet to write *Uncle Tom's Cabin* in 1850. The story of individual slaves was first published in installments in the abolitionist paper, the *Washington National Era*. The first installment was published on June 5, 1851, and the complete work was printed in forty installments over a ten-month period. In March 1852, a Boston publisher printed *Uncle Tom's Cabin* in two volumes. More than 10,000 copies were sold the first week; by 1857, approximately two million copies had been sold worldwide. The book has never been out of print.

Legend says that when President Abraham Lincoln met Harriet Beecher Stowe in 1862, he told her, "So this is the little lady who made this big war." While this may not be true, her book helped to polarize the country on the issue of slavery.

Harriet Beecher Stowe also wrote many nonfiction books. Her subject area was wide ranging, and included books on homemaking and childrearing. She died in Hartford, Connecticut, on July 1, 1896.

Harriet Beecher Stowe

Percentages of Free Families Owning Slaves in Southern States Before the Civil War

Mississippi—49%

South Carolina—46%

Georgia—37%

Alabama—35%

Florida—34%

Louisiana—29%

Texas—28%

North Carolina—28%

Virginia—26%

Tennessee—25%

Kentucky—23%

Arkansas—20%

Missouri—13%

Maryland—12%

Delaware—3%

Harriet Tubman

Two
DIVISIONS BETWEEN NORTH AND SOUTH

As a slave in Maryland, Harriet Tubman did not have an easy life. Although she was married to a free black man, she worried that she would be sold and sent further south. In 1849, her owner died, and she discovered that she and all the other slaves he owned were in fact going to be sold. With the help of a white neighbor, she immediately made her escape. The only person she told she was leaving was her sister; Harriet was afraid that even her husband might betray her.

The neighbor directed Harriet to a house that was a part of the Underground Railroad, smuggling slaves to freedom in the North. From there, Harriet traveled from one house to another, lying in the bottom of a wagon under a rough sack, walking long miles through forests and swamps. Finally, she reached Philadelphia, in the free state of Pennsylvania.

But Harriet was not satisfied with only freeing herself. Over the next twenty years she made nineteen more trips back and forth into slave territory, guiding slaves to freedom. The escaped slaves called her Moses, because she led her people out of slavery.

Moses

Moses is an important figure in Jewish scriptures (the Christian Old Testament). He led the Jewish people out of slavery in Egypt, into the Promised Land where they could be free. African American slaves identified with this story for obvious reasons, and many of their songs referred to the biblical account.

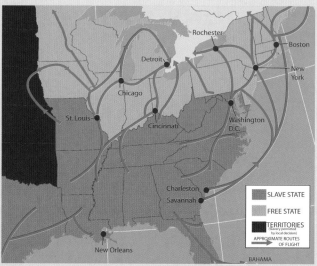

Underground Railroad map

The Underground Railroad was just one symptom of the growing divisions between the Northern and Southern states. The North and the South were very different places. The South, with its large plantations, was a very *agrarian* society. With the popularity of cotton, many of the Southern farmers had even stopped growing food crops. The South found itself dependent on the North for food, for manufactured goods, and for ships to export their cotton to Europe.

For its part, the North enjoyed the prosperity they gained from dealing with the South. The industries and many of the country's businesses were located in the North. Immigrants generally chose to settle in the North, where land was more affordable and there were more jobs. As a result, Northern culture and society kept growing and changing, while Southern culture and society stayed approximately the same.

The South started to resent the power that the North had over them. Their way of life was dependent on the northern part of the country, and they did not have the resources to survive on their own at the same level of well-being. They were angry that the North made money from their plantations and then helped steal their slaves to free them.

The Underground Railroad

The Underground Railroad was a loose network of assistance to people fleeing slavery. Although there was no single, established path, slaves seeking freedom tended to use areas that were known to offer places to hide. These included the area of the Mississippi River and the Appalachian Mountains.

During the 1800s, more than 100,000 slaves used the Underground Railroad in an attempt to find their freedom. Some stayed in the South, where freemen and other slaves helped them. As time progressed, more runaway slaves moved north and found aid along the way with freemen and from whites seeking a method to visibly fight slavery. The Religious Society of Friends—the Quakers—were prominent in the antislavery movement.

Harriet Tubman is perhaps the person most closely associated with the Underground Railroad. A slave herself, Harriet was born around 1822. When she decided to escape to the North, Harriet used the Underground Railroad as she made her way to Philadelphia. Once free, she assisted in bringing about seventy runaways to freedom, and she provided detailed instructions to about fifty more. She spoke out against slavery as well, becoming a well-known abolitionist figure. Harriet Tubman died in Auburn, New York, in 1913.

For the first half of the 1800s, the numbers of slave and free states were equal, and so the North and the South were equally represented in the government. This meant that neither side could override the rights of the other. The Southern slave states worried that if the abolitionists in the North managed to restrict the spread of slavery into the new territories of the West, they would quickly

*An **agrarian** society is one built on farming and agricultural products.*

Nat Turner

Nat Turner was born October 2, 1800, in Southampton County, Virginia. As a young child, his intelligence and ability to describe things that had happened before his birth led many to see the deeply religious Turner as a prophet.

During his life, Turner had many visions. His first, in 1821, occurred after he ran away from his owner. He returned after thirty days because a vision told him that he should. Another vision, on May 12, 1828, told him he should "slay his enemies with their own weapons."

On August 21, 1931, Nat Turner and a small band of followers killed the entire family of his owner while they slept. They moved on, walking from house to house, and killing every white person they met. By this time, the small group had grown to forty slaves, mostly on horses they had stolen. When the group tried to attack another house on August 22, they were met with state and federal troops. Turner escaped, but he was captured on October 30. Turner and his group had stabbed, shot, and beaten at least fifty-five whites to death. He was tried in the Southampton County Courthouse on November 5 and was sentenced to be executed. Nat Turner was hanged, then skinned on November 11.

The state of Virginia executed fifty-five people in the aftermath of the rebellion. The state reimbursed the slaveholders for the slaves. In the heated climate that followed, approximately two hundred blacks, most with no connection to the attacks, were murdered by white mobs. The retaliation was not confined to Virginia. In states as far away as North Carolina, slaves were accused, tried, and executed for having connections with the rebellion. All but a few were innocent.

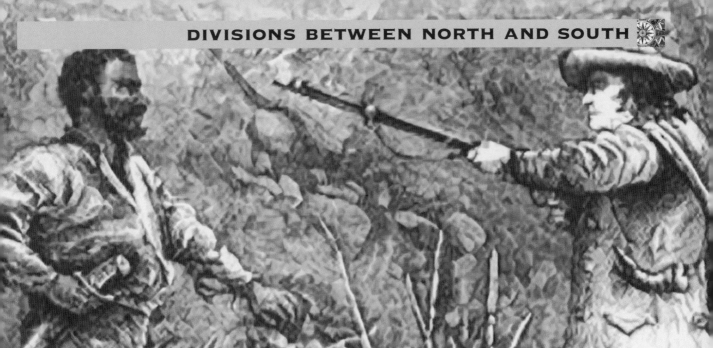

be outnumbered in the Senate.

The clash between *abolitionists* and slave owners had been going on since the American Revolution. Until the 1830s, antislavery societies in the South worked to pass laws that would free the slaves. In 1831, however, a group of slaves led by Nat Turner rebelled and murdered sixty white Virginians. After this, Southern states outlawed antislavery societies and passed stricter slavery laws. These laws made it illegal to teach a slave to read and for

Abolitionists were people who wanted to abolish (or get rid of) slavery.

The capture of Nat Turner

Frederick Douglas, prominent Northern abolishionist

slaves to meet together in groups without a white person being present.

Some slave owners defended the right to own slaves by claiming that the black people were better off in the Christian civilization of America than they had been in the jungles of Africa. Other slaveholders said that they considered their slaves to be part of their families. Although some people truly believed these things, their arguments did not convince the abolitionists.

As America continued to grow and add new territories, the North and South managed to keep the balance of slave and free states. When new slave states joined the Union, an equal number of free states were quickly added as well. In 1820, when Missouri was admitted as a slave state, Maine was admitted as a free state at the same time to keep the balance. The laws that added Missouri and Maine to the Union were called the Missouri Compromise and also included an agreement not to admit any more slave states north of the latitude line of 36° 30', which was Missouri's southern border

The Mexican War, from 1846 to 1848, stirred up the issue of slavery again. With the possibility of gaining new territories, both the South

and the North wanted to make sure their interests were upheld. After the war, Congress passed a series of laws called the Compromise of 1850, designed to satisfy both the North and the South.

Included in the compromise was the Fugitive Slave Act. The Fugitive Slave Act was supposed to make it easier for Southern slave owners to find and retrieve their runaway slaves. Anyone found helping a runaway would be fined heavily or thrown in jail. Government officials would be paid more if they returned the slave to his master than if they freed him. Runaway slaves were not allowed to testify on their own behalf, and they were denied a jury trial.

Northern abolitionists were horrified at the new Fugitive Slave Act. The Underground Railroad worked harder than ever to free slaves and, in several cases, angry mobs intervened to rescue runaways from the people chasing them. The Massachusetts government even went as far as to make it illegal to enforce the new act in their state.

Slave owners in the South were furious. The Fugitive Slave Act had been the only thing of use to them in the Compromise of 1850, and now it was doing them no good at all. To make matters

*A **controversy** is a disagreement between viewpoints.*

*To own **stock** means to have a financial stake in a company.*

worse, the compromise had also granted California statehood as a free state, throwing off the balance between slave and free states.

The new concept of a transcontinental railroad created another **controversy** between the North and the South. Building both northern and southern railroads across the country to the West Coast would be too expensive. The South desperately wanted the advantages that a railroad would bring them: more money, businesses, and people would flow into their region. Southern representatives argued that the proposed route across the South had lower mountains to cross and would pass through more settled regions that were less likely to face Indian attacks. Northerners, on the other hand, reasoned that since thousands of new settlers were rushing to settle in the more northern territory of Nebraska, this would be a better route for the railroad.

In 1854, Senator Stephen Douglas of Illinois took matters into his own hands. He campaigned to have the new railroad start in Chicago, which meant it would take the northerly route west. Douglas wanted to please voters by bringing the railroad to their area, but he also wanted to make money himself, since he owned both land in the area and **stock** in the railroad. To get the South to agree to this proposition, Douglas came up with the Kansas-Nebraska Act.

The Kansas-Nebraska Act stated that the Nebraska territory would be divided into two states, Kansas and Nebraska. Both

Building the transcontinental railroad

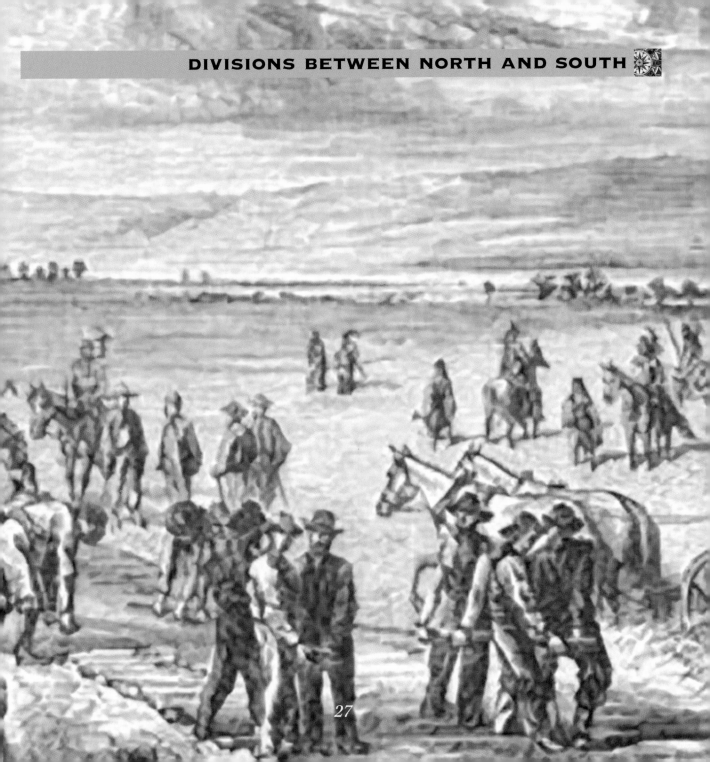

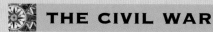
To **repeal** means to do away with a law through government action.

Popular sovereignty means that the government is created by and serves the will of the people; government's power comes from the people.

of these states would be given the right to decide for themselves whether to be slave or free. People assumed that the more southerly Kansas, which bordered the slave state Missouri, would choose to enter the Union as a slave state. Presumably, Nebraska would choose to enter as a free state.

The South quickly agreed to this idea, but there was one problem: the Missouri Compromise had said that no slave states north of Missouri's southern border were to be admitted to the Union as

Stephen Douglas

slave states. Both Kansas and Nebraska were north of this line so, according to the Missouri Compromise, they were only to be admitted as free states.

Eager to pass the Kansas-Nebraska Act and get to work building his railroad, Senator Douglas hurried to get the Missouri Compromise repealed. For three months, the debates raged in Congress. Douglas was a great debater, however, and although the vote was very close, Congress finally **repealed** the Missouri Compromise and passed the Kansas-Nebraska Act into law.

Senator Douglas did not actually feel deeply about the issue of the expansion of slavery. What he cared most about was states' rights, or **popular sovereignty**. He believed very strongly that each state should be able to choose for itself whether to be slave or free. He saw the Missouri Compromise as overriding this choice, and therefore he had no problem with doing away with it.

Other Northerners, however, did not take the Missouri Compromise so lightly. Antislavery groups—such as the Free Soilers—who had taken comfort in the idea that slavery would at least not be allowed to spread north, were horri-

John Brown as he aged

fied at the Kansas-Nebraska Act. Abolitionists rushed to Kansas, bringing weapons and prepared to fight for a free Kansas.

Two years later, conditions in Kansas had gotten much worse. In 1855, groups of both Northern abolitionists and proslavery Southerners tried to set up their own illegal governments. Then, in 1856, violence broke out. First, a proslavery gang attacked and burned part of a free-soil town. Then the abolitionist John Brown

arrived. He had traveled from the Adirondack Mountains of New York State to help in the fight for a free Kansas. Brown and seven of his companions attacked and slaughtered five proslavery men. With that, the violence in Kansas escalated. Bands of rough men from both sides of the issue fought each other throughout the wilderness. They burned houses, stole whatever they could get their hands on, and killed innocent people. Those on the abolitionist side were

John Brown

John Brown was born in 1800 in Torrington, Connecticut, to a deeply religious family. His father was a very vocal abolitionist, and John followed his father's beliefs.

The father of twenty children, John Brown and his family moved many times. Brown had several jobs, but he never found financial success, and he filed for bankruptcy in his forties. However, financial difficulties never stopped him from supporting the abolitionist cause. He even moved to the black community of North Elba, New York, in 1849. He wanted to be a role model for black farmers there.

Although he was always an abolitionist, John Brown did not become a well-known figure until 1855. It was then that he followed some of his sons to the Kansas territory and became a leader in the anti-slavery rebellion.

Brown returned to the East and hatched the plan that became the attack on Harpers Ferry, Virginia. On October 16, 1859, Brown led twenty-one men (five blacks and sixteen whites) on a raid on the federal arsenal there. His plan was to arm slaves with the weapons they had seized. The raid was stopped by local farmers, militiamen, and the Marines, who were led by Robert E. Lee. Most of Brown's men were killed or captured within thirty-six days. Brown, himself, was wounded and captured easily. He was moved to Charlestown, Virginia, where he was tried and convicted of treason. John Brown was hanged on December 2, 1859.

Constituents are the people who those in government are elected to represent.

Reward for the return of a runaway slave

called Jayhawkers and those on the slavery side were called Bushwhackers.

Shocked by what was happening in Kansas, Massachusetts Senator Charles Sumner, an outspoken abolitionist, gave a speech in Congress in May of 1856 called "The Crime Against Kansas." Sumner blamed the South—and specifically South Carolina Senator Andrew Butler—for attempting to force Kansas into becoming a slave state against the wishes of most of the people who lived there. Sumner's speech was fiery and biting. He criticized Senator Butler's association with slavery, as well as called him a liar. "He shows an incapacity of accuracy," Sumner said. "He cannot open his mouth, but out there flies a blunder."

Senator Butler was not in Congress when Sumner gave his speech, but his nephew, Representative Preston Brooks of South Carolina, was there. Brooks took the speech as a personal insult against his family. Two days after the speech, Brooks walked into the Senate chamber where Senator Sumner was writing at his desk and attacked him with a walking stick. Brooks hit the senator on the head until his cane splintered and two other congressmen finally were able to pull him away. Sumner was unconscious after the attack; he spent the next three and a half years in Europe recovering from severe head injuries. Brooks resigned from the House of Representatives, but his actions were so popular with his *constituents* that they immediately reelected him.

Northerners were outraged by the assault on Senator Sumner. As far as they were concerned, Brooks was a coward and a bully. In the North, the attack became an image of the cruelty of Southern slave owners. If a gentleman politician would beat a respected col-

Charles Sumner

league over the head with a stick, how must he and those who applauded his actions treat their slaves?

Abraham Lincoln, a reenactment

34

Presidents in the 20 years before the Civil War

John Tyler (1841–1845), Whig

Although he feared it would mean the spread of slavery, he made Texas a state three days before he left office as President.

James Knox Polk (1845–1849), Democrat

He wanted more than anything to expand the Union. He fought the Mexican War and acquired the land that now makes up California, Nevada, Utah, Arizona, and Texas.

Zachary Taylor (1849–1850), Whig

He had been a war hero of the Mexican War. He threatened to veto any compromises that would allow the spread of slavery to the western territories, but he died before he had the chance.

Millard Fillmore (1850–1853), Whig

He was Zachary Taylor's Vice President. He quickly signed the Compromise of 1850 when he became President.

Franklin Pierce (1853–1857), Democrat

He was not a decisive or forceful man. He won the election because the Whig Party was divided and split over the slavery issue. Pierce's cabinet members were both decisive and forceful, however. They convinced him to sign the Kansas-Nebraska Act, as well as to try to take over Cuba and make it a slave state.

James Buchanan (1857–1861), Democrat

He was an uncertain and vague man and never really understood how divided the country had actually become. He thought the problems between the North and South would probably just go away.

Abraham Lincoln (1861–1865), Republican

The South seceded when he was elected, rather than accept an antislavery Republican as President.

Abraham Lincoln

Three
SECESSION OF THE SOUTH

Abraham Lincoln was a tall, gaunt man, with a sad, sunken face. At six feet, four inches tall, he towered over most of the men of his day. His arms and legs were long and thin, and most of his height came from the length of his legs; when he sat down, he was not any taller than other men. He had unusually large hands and rough, black hair that was hard to comb neatly. Pictures usually show him with a full, dark beard, but for most of his life he was cleanshaven. He did not grow his famous beard until about the time he became President, when an eleven-year-old girl from western New York wrote him a letter suggesting he "would look a great deal better" with a beard, since his face was so thin.

Lincoln was born in a log cabin in the Kentucky woods and moved to southern Indiana when he was seven years old. Although he went to a *frontier* school for a short time, he was mostly self-taught. He read everything he could get his hands on and frustrated his father because he would rather borrow books from the neighbors and read than work in the fields.

*The **frontier** was a region that had not yet been settled.*

38

In 1830, he moved with his family to Illinois, worked as a storekeeper and postmaster (among other things), and read law books in his spare time. Six years later, he passed the bar exam and became a lawyer. Almost immediately, he acquired the nickname "Honest Abe," because he refused to defend law clients he thought were guilty. Abe carried his important papers in his stovepipe hat so he would not lose them, a habit he continued even as President. During the 1830s and 1840s, he was active as a politician in Illinois, but he then retired from politics to concentrate on his law practice and raising his family.

Abraham Lincoln

The Kansas-Nebraska Act in 1854 disturbed Lincoln so much that he decided to get back into politics. In 1856, he joined the new Republican Party. The Republican Party had been formed by people from several different existing parties—the Northern Whigs, the Free Soil Party, the Know-Nothings, and even some unhappy Democrats—who came together with the common goal of stopping the spread of slavery.

In the 1858 Illinois Senate race, Lincoln ran as a Republican against Stephen Douglas. Douglas, a Democrat, had been the author of the controversial Kansas-Nebraska Act. For two months in the fall of 1858, Lincoln and Douglas held a series of debates in which they argued about the expansion of slavery. Douglas argued that the Union could exist with both slave and free states. Lincoln, on the other hand, said: "'A house divided against itself cannot stand.' I believe this government cannot endure permanently half slave and half free. I do not expect the Union to be dissolved—I do not expect the house to fall—but I do expect it will cease to be divided. It will become all one thing, or all the other."

Lincoln lost the Senate election to Douglas, but the nation had noticed him. In 1860, the Republican Party chose him as their presidential candidate. The South, however, barely acknowledged the existence of the new Republican Party. The Republicans were running on a *platform* that was directly contrary to the Southern way of thinking and way of life, and the South refused to even put the Republicans on the ballot for the election. South Carolina threatened to *secede* from the Union if Lincoln was elected.

The gulf between North and South had been growing increasingly wider for almost a century. The South had been on the road to secession for a long time, but the election of Abraham Lincoln to the presidency was the final blow.

As soon as South Carolina realized that Lincoln had been elected, they called together a group of *delegates* to vote on secession. With a unanimous vote of 169 to zero, South Carolina seceded from the United States on December 20, 1860. In their Declaration of Secession, they wrote:

> A geographical line has been drawn across the Union, and all the States north of that line have united in the election of a man to the high office of President of the United States, whose opinions and purposes are hostile to slavery. He is to be entrusted with the administration of the common Government, because he has declared that that "Government cannot endure permanently half slave, half free," and that the public mind must rest in the belief that slavery is in the course of ultimate extinction.

South Carolina was followed by Mississippi (January 9, 1861), Florida (January 10), Alabama (January 11), Georgia (January 19), Louisiana (January 26), and Texas (February 1).

In February of 1861, these Southern states met and formed the Confederate States of America, naming Jefferson Davis their president. Davis had been a senator from Mississippi before the secession. He was not at the meeting

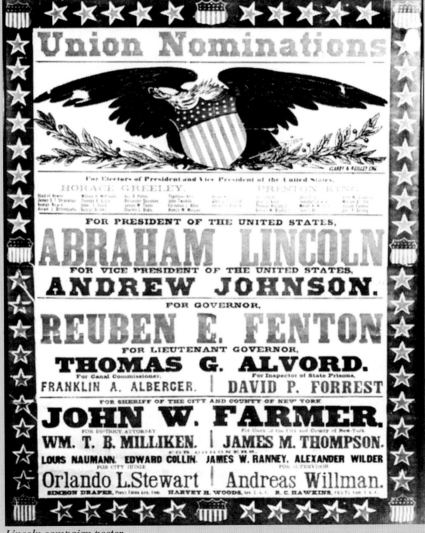

Lincoln campaign poster

*A political **platform** is a declaration of principles on which a group or individual stands.*

*To **secede** means to break away from.*

***Delegates** are representatives chosen to represent a group of people.*

41

when he was named president and he would have preferred to be a part of the Confederate army, but he accepted the presidency.

Although Abraham Lincoln had been elected as President of the United States, he did not officially take office until March 4, 1861. Meanwhile, President Buchanan did nothing about the secession of the Southern states. He did not want the Union to be divided, and he did not think the South was acting legally in declaring itself independent, but he did not think that the U.S. Constitution gave him any power to stop the Southern states.

A New York political gathering

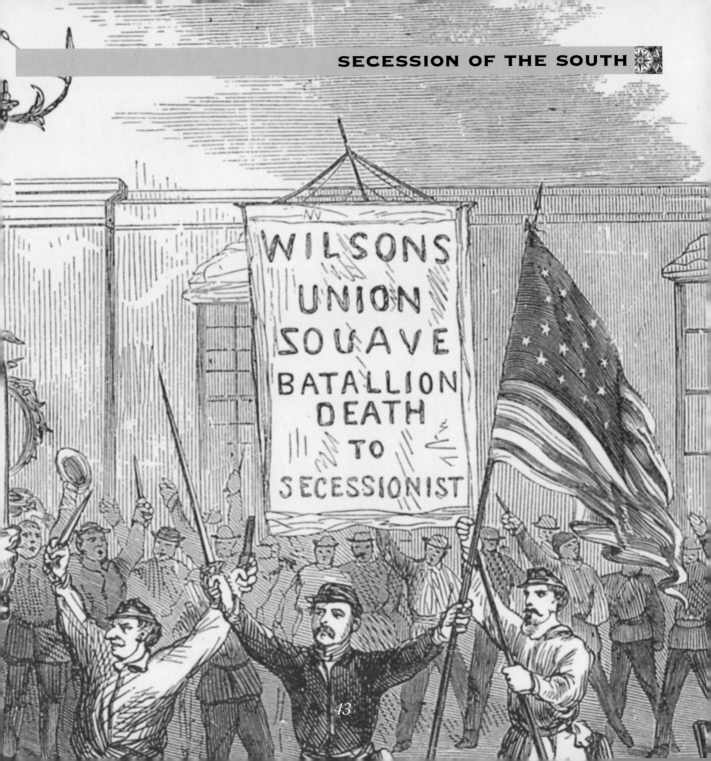

Abraham Lincoln and his advisors

The Confederacy did not believe the North would go to war against them either. They saw their actions as being similar to those of the colonies in 1776, when they declared their independence from Britain. They also thought that the North would be unwilling to give up the money they made selling Southern cotton to Europe, as they would have to do if war was declared.

LATEST FROM
CHARLESTON

SUMTER ON FIRE!!

REBELS FIRING ON

THE BURNING FORT!!

The news from Charleston, Virginia

In his **_inaugural_** speech as President, Lincoln argued that the Southern states could not legally secede and assured them that he was simply against the expansion of slavery, not for its entire abolition. He ended his speech by reassuring them once again that he wanted to preserve the Union and prevent war:

> In your hands, my dissatisfied fellow-countrymen, and not in mine, is the momentous issue of civil war. The Government will not assail you. You can have no conflict without being yourselves the aggressors. You have no oath registered in heaven to destroy the Government, while I shall have the most solemn one to "preserve, protect, and defend it."

By the time Lincoln took office, only two forts in the South remained loyal to the Union. Lincoln discovered that one of these, Fort Sumter in the Charleston harbor, could not hold out without more supplies. Lincoln sent a message to the Confederate government telling them that he was sending provisions but no reinforcements. He hoped that by notifying them, he would avoid conflict.

***Inaugural** means swearing in to office.*

Maryland did not leave the Union, but many of its citizens were pro-South. Civilians in the streets of Baltimore attacked the Northern troops

Map of Charleston Harbor

The battle of Fort Sumter marked the beginning of the Civil War. Up until this point, many Northerners were willing to see the South secede. The attack on their fort, however, stirred up emotions and patriotic feelings. Northerners were now eager to follow Lincoln into the South to fight for the preservation of their country.

Southern states that had not seceded earlier found themselves faced with a decision. They realized that war was becoming unavoidable. Virginia, Arkansas, and Tennessee all joined the Confederacy in the early months of the war. Part of Virginia did not want to secede, though, and broke away to become West Virginia at this time.

Lincoln was able to prevent the Border States—Delaware, Missouri, Kentucky, and Maryland, slave states that shared borders with free states—from seceding by arguing that he was going to war only to preserve the Union. In the early part of the war, he avoided any discussion of slavery whenever possible. By not talking about outlawing slavery, Lincoln won the support of these states and kept them from joining the other slave states in the Confederacy.

The Confederacy was suspicious, however. They moved quickly to try and force the surrender of Fort Sumter's commander. When the commander refused to surrender immediately, South Carolina attacked the fort. The Union forces at Fort Sumter surrendered on April 12, 1861, and South Carolina took control of the fort.

A sergeant restoring the stars and stripes to the ramparts of Fort Sumter before the final fall of the fort to the Confederates

Four
THE CIVIL WAR

Robert E. Lee was serving as a colonel in the U.S. Army in Texas when word reached him that the South had seceded from the Union. Lee had been following the developing crisis between the North and South carefully, but he had not expected events to move so quickly. With the news of the secession came orders that Lee was to return to Washington. Colonel Lee knew what these orders probably meant. He expected he was being called up to take part in bringing the Southern rebels back into the Union—and he was right. He had thought a long time about this situation, and he had prayed hard that it would never happen. Now that it had, he had to make a choice.

The Civil War,
a reenactment

Lee was a Southern gentleman who believed strongly in honor and duty. He did not strongly support slavery, though, and he once claimed that if he owned all the slaves in the South he would free them to keep the Union together. Lee was very loyal to the Union, but he was more loyal to his native Virginia. He thought of his fellow Virginians as his family. When Virginia seceded, as he had feared it would, he resigned from the U.S. Army rather than fight against his state. He wrote to his sister, who lived in the North, to try and explain why he had resigned:

> With all my devotion to the Union and the feeling of loyalty and duty of an American citizen, I have not been able to make up my mind to raise my hand against my relatives, my children, my home. I have therefore resigned my commission in the Army, and save in defense of my native State, with the sincere hope that my poor services may never be needed, I hope I may never be called on to draw my sword.

Although Lee was hoping that he would not be forced to fight at all, and that Virginia would be able to remain neutral in the conflict between the North and the South, he did not get his wish. When Virginia chose to join with the Confederacy and asked Lee to help lead their army, he agreed. Lee's loyalty to Virginia was so strong that even though he did not want to fight against the Union armies, when his state asked him to fight he never considered refusing.

The Civil War was a terrible experience for both the North and the South. It is sometimes called the Brothers War because allegiances were split even among families. One brother would fight for the North, while another fought for the South. Even Abraham Lincoln's wife had four brothers who fought for the Confederate army.

At the beginning, no one thought the war would be as long or as destructive as it was. The North was **optimistic** that they could easily defeat the Confederacy. Lincoln decided that an attack on the Southern forces at Bull Run would show the Confederates the superior strength they would be up against if they continued to pursue secession. Thousands of eager young men arrived to fight for the North, proud and elegant in their new uniforms. Most of them believed that this would be the only battle of the war and they were thrilled to be able to help defeat the upstart Confederates. Members of Congress packed picnic lunches and rode down

Robert E. Lee

Optimistic *means expecting the best of a situation.*

Confederate uniform

Confederate buttons and buckles

from Washington with their families to watch the battle from an overlooking hill.

Defeating the South was not as easy as the Union army had hoped, however. Instead of facing the disorganized and inexperienced troops they were expecting, the Northerners came face to face with Stonewall Jackson, who was neither disorganized nor inexperienced. The battle they had thought would give them a few hours of entertainment turned brutal as the fighting went on for hours. Nine hundred men died at the first battle of Bull Run. Suddenly, the North realized they were in for a much longer struggle than they had anticipated.

The Civil War is sometimes thought to be the first real "total war" in history. A total war is one in which both sides use all their resources to try and destroy the ability of their opponent to wage war. The War Between the States became an expensive battle that tested which side was financially more prepared to fight a war that dragged on for years.

The North, whose economy was built on both farming and factories, was clearly better able to survive such a war. They could make weapons and uniforms for their soldiers, as well as grow food to feed them. The North had better

Stonewall Jackson

railroads to transport men and equipment quickly to where they were needed. Besides this, most of the battles were fought on Southern territory, which left Northern towns undisturbed by the actual fighting and better able to continue producing food and equipment.

The South hoped that by claiming its independence as a new country they could attract the attention, and ultimately the support, of

The Union army

Europe. Britain relied on the South for large quantities of cotton, and the Confederacy calculated that this dependence would make the English more likely to offer aid. Most Britons, however, believed that slavery was morally evil. Even if some of the ruling aristocrats were sympathetic to the Southern cause, they were not prepared to risk mob riots by their outraged citizens if they allied themselves with the Confederacy. Besides, the cotton the Confederates expected would tie Britain to them turned out not to be such an influencing factor after all: a surplus of cotton had built up in British warehouses, and when those stores ran low after several years, the British turned to India and Egypt to meet their cotton needs. The South was forced to fight the war without any direct European support.

The North did not hold all the advantages, however. The South had better officers, such as Robert E. Lee and Stonewall Jackson, and their men, in general, were better prepared to be soldiers than those in the North. Thousands of men had quickly volunteered to fight for the Northern armies after the attack on Fort Sumter, but most of them were unprepared for military life. The Union also had to deal with numerous incompetent leaders before Lincoln found Ulysses S. Grant and put him in charge of the Union armies in 1864, three years after the start of the war.

Although the main cause of the Civil War was slavery, for the first year, Lincoln continued to claim that the Union armies were not fighting to free the slaves. The reason for the war, he said, was to keep the country together. Lincoln was

Confederate flag and weapons

afraid that if he mentioned slavery, the north-ernmost slave states—Maryland, Delaware, Kentucky, and Missouri—would join with the Confederacy. It was clear, however, that the United States could not continue to be partly slave and partly free. The issue of slavery had been causing serious problems for decades, and it would have to be resolved if the country was to stay together.

Lincoln waited until his Union armies won their first major battle of the war, the Battle of Antietam, to mention the issue of slavery. It was not an overwhelming victory, but it was enough that Lincoln felt he could now bring up the subject

Civil War battle

without fearing the Border States would secede. Less than a week after the battle, on September 22, 1862, Lincoln issued the Emancipation Proclamation, which then went into effect on January 1, 1863. The Emancipation Proclamation set free all slaves from Confederate States. Although no slaves were immediately affected by the proclamation, it was the first step toward the complete abolition of slavery in America.

The Emancipation Proclamation gave the war a new direction. The South now knew they could not hope to reenter the Union and go back to the way things had been. The North now had a strong moral reason to keep fighting. Although there were some desertions among Union soldiers who were not in favor of abolishing slavery, who had joined the army to fight to keep the country together, overall, the Emancipation Proclamation was a good thing for Northern forces, and they fought their battles with a new sense of morality.

One of the most famous of these battles was the Battle of Gettysburg. The battle, which took place in July of 1863 near Gettysburg, Pennsylvania, lasted for three days. It was the largest battle ever fought in the Western Hemisphere and was the turning point of the Civil War.

Until this time, Robert E. Lee's Confederate army had been a huge problem for the Union forces. Lee and his forces had fought most of the battles won by the South. This time, though, several of Lee's commanders had been recently promoted and were working under General Lee for the first time. Lee had a habit of leaving many of the details of an attack up to his commanders. This style of commanding had succeeded well when he was working with Stonewall Jackson, but Jackson had died after the Battle of Chancellorsville earlier that spring.

For two days the Union and Confederate armies fought, with no clear winner. On the third and final day of the battle, General George Pickett led his men in a charge across a huge expanse of open ground toward the line of Union forces. Although the charge temporarily broke the Northerners' line of defense, the attackers were driven back after losing three-quarters of their men.

Pickett's Charge was the turning point of both the battle and the war. Until then, the South had not really thought they would be beaten. Gettysburg was a terrible battle; alto-

A Proclamation.

Whereas, on the twenty-second day of September, in the year of our Lord one thousand eight hundred and sixty-two, a proclamation was issued by the President of the United States, containing, among other things, the following, to wit:

"That on the first day of January, in the year of our Lord one thousand eight hundred and sixty-three, all persons held as slaves within any State or designated part of a State, the people whereof shall then be in rebellion against the

61

Invincible means being incapable of losing or being injured or killed.

gether, there were 51,000 casualties in both the Northern and the Southern forces. Pickett's ineffective charge against the Northern forces represented both the South's optimistic belief that they were *invincible* and the fact that they were not.

The Gettysburg Address

Four score and seven years ago our fathers brought forth on this continent a new nation, conceived in liberty and dedicated to the proposition that all men are created equal. Now we are engaged in a great civil war, testing whether that nation, or any nation so conceived and so dedicated, can long endure. We are met on a great battlefield of that war. We have come to dedicate a portion of that field, as a final resting place for those who here gave their lives that that nation might live. It is altogether fitting and proper that we should do this.

But, in a larger sense, we cannot dedicate—we cannot consecrate—we cannot hallow—this ground. The brave men, living and dead, who struggled here, have consecrated it, far above our poor power to add or detract. The world will little note, nor long remember what we say here, but it can never forget what they did here. It is for us the living, rather, to be dedicated here to the unfinished work which they who fought here have thus far so nobly advanced. It is rather for us to be here dedicated to the great task remaining before us—that from these honored dead we take increased devotion to that cause for which they gave the last full measure of devotion—that we here highly resolve that these dead shall not have died in vain—that this nation, under God, shall have a new birth of freedom—and that government of the people, by the people, for the people, shall not perish from the earth.

Gettysburg National Monument today

In the November following the battle, President Lincoln traveled to Gettysburg to dedicate the Soldiers' National Cemetery. The speech he gave at the dedication, the Gettysburg Address, has become Lincoln's most famous speech, even though the people at the time were not very impressed with it. The Gettysburg Address acknowledged the sacrifice made by the men of both the North and the South and again emphasized the struggle of the war to keep the nation together.

The greatest of the Union generals, Ulysses S. Grant, had fought in the Mexican War and then resigned in order to avoid being court-martialed for drunkenness. When the Civil War began, Grant reenlisted and was quickly promoted through the ranks as his talent and ability was recognized. President Lincoln noticed Grant's successes and finally, having gone through a number of unsatisfactory generals, promoted Grant to general and put him in charge of all the Union armies in March of 1864.

Grant gave his friend General William T. Sherman the job of capturing Georgia. Sherman was a forceful and blunt man. He hated war, but he believed that it was necessary. He fought brutally to win and to win as quickly as possible. Sherman's famous March to the Sea in the late fall of 1864 was an extremely destructive and effective military campaign. Sherman burned houses, fields, and entire towns, including Atlanta. His purpose was both to destroy resources that the Confederate Army could use and to destroy the morale and will of the Southern people to fight. In December,

Sherman reached Savannah and sent a letter to President Lincoln offering him the city as a Christmas gift.

While Sherman took Georgia, Grant faced Robert E. Lee and his Confederate armies near Richmond, Virginia. Early in April 1865, General Lee finally abandoned Richmond to the Union forces and withdrew to the village of Appomattox Courthouse. Here, Grant was able to surround the Southern forces and, on April 9, 1865, Lee surrendered.

With Lee's surrender, the war was basically over. Within several months, all the South's forces had surrendered. War had exhausted the Confederacy and drained their economy. They were no longer in any condition to keep fighting.

That summer, Lee applied for an official pardon from the President. He accepted that he must submit to the authority of the United States government. General Grant also wrote a letter recommending that Lee be granted this pardon. Although the pardon was never granted, the fact that Lee had applied for it encouraged many former Confederates to apply for pardons and to accept their place in the reunited nation.

Sherman destroyed homes throughout the South, as well as farms, businesses, and entire towns. This is an actual photograph of a Southern town after Sherman's destruction.

Five
RECONSTRUCTION

Ford's Theatre was packed on the night of April 14, 1865. The play was a popular comedy, *Our American Cousin*, and this was its final performance in Washington. It was Good Friday, but this year the usual solemn mood of Holy Week was offset by excitement. The war was over!

The newspapers had reported that General Grant would be going to the play with President Lincoln, and everyone wanted to get a look at the men responsible for winning the war. As it happened, however, Grant did not go to the theatre with Lincoln after all. He and his wife left Washington early that evening to visit their children in New Jersey.

President Lincoln sat in a box overlooking the stage of the theatre, along with his wife, Mary Todd Lincoln, and some friends. The crowd was spirited that night, laughing at the play's comical characters and applauding loudly when the actors ad-libbed lines about the end of the war and the President.

Ford's Theatre

Lincoln and son Tad

Lincoln's box at Ford's Theatre

John Wilkes Booth, an actor, was also in Ford's Theatre that night, although he was not in the play. Booth hated President Lincoln. He had supported the Confederacy, and he was angry that the Northern forces had won the war. A month earlier, Booth and others who shared his feelings had made plans to kidnap the President at an appearance just outside Washington and to then exchange him for Confederate prisoners. The plan had failed when Lincoln cancelled his trip at the last moment.

This time, Booth was determined not to fail. He had spent hours that day planning his at-tack. He knew every word of the play being per-formed at Ford's Theater and which lines made the audience laugh the loudest. He calculated that at approximately 10:15 that night, the play would be part way through its final act. At that time, only one actor would be on the stage, and he would deliver a line that always caused the audience to roar with laughter. Booth hoped that the laughter would be enough to cover the sound of a gunshot.

At a little after ten that night, Booth arrived at the theatre, leaving his horse in the back alley. He waited outside Lincoln's box until he heard the actor start to speak the line Booth was an-ticipating. Quietly, he opened the door and slipped inside the darkened box, drawing his gun as he did so. When the audience erupted in laughter, Booth put the gun to Lincoln's head and pulled the trigger.

After shooting the President, Booth leapt from the box onto the stage, breaking his leg when he landed. In the confusion, he managed to escape to his horse through a back door. The next day, he was shot and killed when soldiers tracked him down and tried to arrest him.

President Lincoln was carried unconscious to a house across the road from the theater. He

never regained consciousness and died the next morning.

Booth had intended that Vice President Andrew Johnson, and Secretary of State William Seward be assassinated at the same time as Lincoln. He had assigned men to kill Johnson and Seward, but the man sent to kill Seward had only managed to wound him. The man Booth had sent to kill the Vice President had not been very enthusiastic about the plan to begin with and did not make any attempt to assassinate Johnson.

By assassinating the three most important men in Washington, Booth had hoped to throw the government into *chaos*. Then, he thought, perhaps the Confederacy might be able to seize the opportunity to reorganize itself and escape defeat.

Although Lincoln's death did not have the effect Booth had intended, it did make the ***reconstruction*** of the country much more difficult. For one thing, many Northerners thought that Jefferson Davis, the president of the Confederacy, had planned the attack. They were already angry with the South, but Lincoln's assassination made them even more hostile toward the Southerners.

After Lincoln died, his Vice President, Andrew Johnson, was sworn in as President. Although Johnson had many good qualities, he was not as suited to dealing with the issues that arose in the years after the Civil War as Lincoln would have been. Neither the Northerners nor the Southerners trusted Johnson completely, and he faced continual conflicts with Congress and even with his own ***cabinet*** members.

Even before the war ended, Lincoln had created a plan for bringing the Southern states back into the Union. Lincoln's plan required 10 percent of voters in a Southern state to swear allegiance to the Union and the state to agree to enforce the Emancipation Proclamation and free their slaves. If these condi-

Chaos *means a disorganized mess.*

Reconstruction *is the act of rebuilding something that has been torn down or destroyed.*

A ***cabinet*** *is a government leader's body of advisors.*

John Wilkes Booth fleeing Ford's Theatre

71

*To **veto** means to reject.*

tions were met, the state was to be readmitted to the Union. Congress was worried that Lincoln's conditions were not strict enough, however. Many congressmen thought that more people should be required to swear allegiance to the Union, and they feared that under Lincoln's plan, rich Southerners would find ways to keep their slaves.

For the most part, Johnson followed Lincoln's plan for readmitting the Southern states. He did add stricter requirements for some of the wealthier Southern states, however. Johnson had grown up as a poor boy, and he enjoyed making so many rich and

Freed African Americans in Richmond

powerful men appeal to him for something they needed.

One of the biggest issues the United States faced after the Civil War was how to deal with the freed slaves. In 1865, Congress established the Freedmen's Bureau to help provide both black and white people of the South with food, clothes, medical care, and education. Some Southern whites, though, thwarted the efforts of the Freedman's Bureau and managed to trick freed slaves into signing labor contracts that made them little better than the slaves they had been.

After they were readmitted to the Union, Southern states created "Black Codes" to try and keep control over the black population. The details of the codes differed slightly among states, but all of them limited the freedoms of African Americans and tried to force them into continuing in their former slave roles. The Black Codes angered the North; it seemed to them that slavery was continuing under another name, and they wondered if they had fought the war for nothing.

In 1866, Congress outlawed the Black Codes and moved to pass a Civil Rights Bill that would give citizenship to the freed slaves. President Johnson *vetoed* the bill, but Congress overrode his veto and passed the bill anyway.

On March 2, 1867, Congress passed the Reconstruction Act and did away with the Southern state governments that had been established since the end of the Civil War. The South was divided into five districts. A Union general governed each district, accompanied by thousands of Union soldiers to keep order.

Under the Reconstruction Act, Southern states needed to grant the freed slaves citizenship and give all adult black men the right to vote. To make sure the South did not try to take away voting rights from African Americans, Congress passed the Fifteenth Amendment guaranteeing voting rights to all adult black men.

The South was in an upheaval after the Civil War. Hundreds of thousands of freedmen were struggling to find their place in society, while former slave owners adjusted to life without slaves. A number of black men enthusiastically used their new freedom to get involved with politics. In the Reconstruction years, black men were elected as mayors, congressmen, senators, lieutenant governors, magistrates, sheriffs, and justices of the peace.

When Southern states reentered the Union they were reorganized with Republican governments. The Republican Party had begun as a strongly abolitionist party and had been hated by the proslavery Southern Democrats before the war. Now, the war was over and the Republican Party was in control of the government in Washington. Since the federal government was in control of the South, the new state governments were set up as Republican.

Northerners traveled south and joined the new state Republican parties. The Southerners called these newcomers carpetbaggers because they arrived with everything they owned packed into suitcases made of carpet. The carpetbaggers found ways to get themselves elected into the disorganized Southern governments and then used their power to steal from the people. Apart from the carpetbaggers, the South also had to deal with the scalawags. The scalawags

were white Southern politicians who joined the new Republican governments and stole from their fellow countrymen. Some Southerners joined the Republicans because they sincerely believed that adapting to the changes taking place in their country was the best thing to do. Scalawags, though, were corrupt and took money from the state treasuries, robbing their impoverished neighbors.

One of the worst examples of a scalawag was Colonel Franklin J. Moses, Jr. Moses had been strongly in support of secession and had, in fact, been the man to raise the Confederate flag over Fort Sumter in 1861, after the battle that began the Civil War. When the war was over, Moses joined the Republican Party and was elected governor of South Carolina. As governor, how-

75

White supremacists believe that people with white skin are superior to all other people.

Literacy is the ability to read and write.

*To **impeach** means to charge a public official with a crime or misconduct in office.*

*When someone is **acquitted** he is found not guilty.*

*A **precedent** is something that is said or done that can be used as the basis for future legal actions.*

ever, instead of using his position to help rebuild the damaged state, he stole money from the state treasury.

With so many black men gaining political power in the South, some whites started to feel threatened. They were used to black people being slaves—working in their cotton fields and serving in their plantation homes. Now, these former slaves were suddenly in positions of power over them. Angry at the changes taking place in their society, some white men started to form secret groups like the Ku Klux Klan. The men of the Ku Klux Klan wore white sheets and tried to scare successful freedmen. When scaring the former slaves didn't work, the **white supremacists** sometimes beat or killed them.

The activities of groups like the Ku Klux Klan prompted laws in the 1870s to protect blacks from hostile white racists. Even after this, however, some whites found ways to oppress their black neighbors, such as making **literacy** a requirement for voting and then giving literacy tests to the poorly educated blacks. In this way, they kept many black men from being allowed to vote.

In 1868, the United States suffered another blow when the House of Representatives tried to impeach President Johnson. Johnson had not gotten along well with Congress ever since he had become President. Some of the Radical Republicans in Congress, unhappy with how Johnson was handling the Reconstruction of the South, had gotten the secretary of war, Edwin M. Stanton, to agree to spy on him. To make sure that Johnson did not fire Stanton, Congress passed the Tenure of Office Act. This act said that the President could not fire any appointees once Congress had approved them, unless the Senate agreed. Johnson tried to veto the act, but Congress over-rode him.

Johnson must have been suspicious, because early in 1868 he fired Stanton in spite of the act. This was the excuse Congress had been waiting for. They charged Johnson with "high crimes and misdemeanors," including breaking the Tenure of Office Act, and with verbally abusing members of Congress.

The American public found the **impeachment** extremely exciting. The trial became entertainment, with tickets sold to the curious crowd. In spite of the attempts of the Radicals, however, Johnson was **acquitted** in the Senate. In order to remove the President from office, at least two-thirds of the Senate would have needed to vote that he was guilty. Although they did not like Johnson, the Senate realized the seriousness of removing a President. Such action, without a very good reason, would weaken the government and set a dangerous precedent for the future.

The year of the impeachment, 1868, was also an election year. Johnson did not run for reelection, and the Republican Party chose General Ulysses S. Grant as their presidential candidate. Grant was a popular war hero, and the Republi-

Cartoon representing the difficulties in the South after the war

cans used that fact to their advantage. One Republican election slogan was "Vote as You Shot," which encouraged people to remember their experiences in the Civil War.

Grant won the election, but he turned out to have been a better general than he was a President. While Grant was in office, the country faced a number of corruption scandals. Politicians at various levels seemed intent on using their positions to cheat the American people. Grant was reelected in the next presi-

Ticket to Andrew Johnson's impeachment

dential election, in 1872, but only because the public thought that his opponent, Horace Greeley, was even worse than he was. Grant seems to have been innocent of corruption himself, but many of the people around him were not. Grant's worst problem was that he did not notice character flaws in those around him until it was too late. He also had difficulty dealing with the scandals that arose during his presidency. Too often he ignored the issues or dealt with them halfheartedly instead of taking strong steps to prevent further corruption.

When he left the White House, he told the people, "Failures have been errors of judgment, not of intent."

During Grant's time as President, the country was still reeling from the effects of the Civil War. The political corruption that ran throughout both the North and the South was a symptom of the still-disorganized nation. As the Reconstruction years passed, however, the upheaval of American society began to calm. The United States was starting to become one nation again.

Boss Tweed

One of the worst cases of political corruption during Grant's administration was that of Boss Tweed. William Marcy Tweed began his political career as an alderman in New York City in 1851. Over the next fifteen years, he worked his way up through the Democratic Party in New York until, by 1868, he was a New York State Senator. Tweed essentially had control of the whole Democratic Party in the state of New York, choosing the nominees and appointees for political positions. Through a corrupt system of granting special favors, he controlled the voters as well. Poor people came to Tweed and his followers for jobs and handouts, which gave them a reason to make sure Tweed stayed in power.

Boss Tweed

Besides giving money and jobs to those who supported him, Tweed also stole from the New York City Treasury. In the time from 1865 to 1871, Tweed stole between twenty million and two hundred million dollars.

When he was exposed, Tweed was convicted and then sued by New York State for six million dollars. He was put in debtor's prison, but he escaped in 1875. For nearly a year he kept his freedom, working as a seaman on a Spanish ship. Then, in 1876, he was recognized—allegedly from a political cartoon—and returned to prison in New York. He died in prison two years later.

Six
THE NATION REUNITED

One hundred years had passed since the thirteen original American colonies had declared their independence from Britain and formed the United States of America. In those hundred years, the country had already faced two major wars: the first for their independence, the second—the Civil War—to keep the nation together and bring freedom to the black slaves in the South. In 1876, the Union had been reunited, but that year brought another political scandal to the nation.

Before the presidential election of 1876, the Republican Party was split, with each group trying to get their man nominated as the Republican candidate. The "Stalwart" group backed United States Senator Roscoe Conkling, while the "Half-Breeds" put forward James G. Blaine. Finally, the groups compromised and chose Ohio governor Rutherford B. Hayes as the Republican candidate. The Republican convention at which Hayes was nominated was controversial, with angry rivals trying to discredit each other with charges of corruption. The controversy of the convention, however, was completely overshadowed by the election scandal that followed.

Monument on Little Roundtop
commemorating Civil War battles

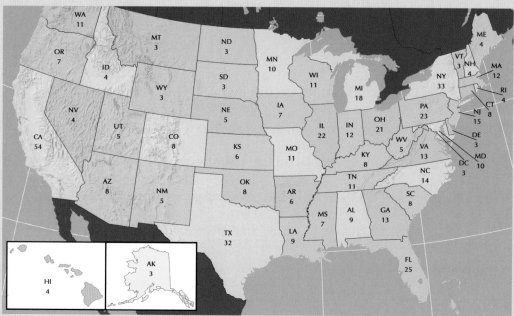

Modern electoral college map

Hayes ran against Samuel J. Tilden, the Democratic candidate. Tilden was an attorney famous for prosecuting the corrupt politician Boss Tweed, and in his campaign he promised reforms that would rid the country of political scandals.

To win the election, a candidate needed to receive 185 electoral votes. When the results were counted, although Tilden had won the popular vote by 250,000, he had only 184 elec-toral votes. Hayes had 165, and twenty electoral votes were in dispute. The twenty disputed votes came from four different states—South Carolina, Louisiana, Florida, and Oregon. In each case, both the Republicans and the Democrats claimed to have won.

For months, the outcome of the election was in question. Early in 1877, the Electoral Count Act was passed. Under the act, a commission of fifteen men from the Senate, House of

The Constitutional Convention, 1787

One of the issues facing the Constitutional Convention was the best way to elect the President. Congress could choose the President—but this was rejected because of the concern that it could lead to corruption or upset the balance of power. Another method considered was for the state legislatures to elect the president. Many felt that this would erode federal authority. The last option was election through direct popular vote. The Constitutional Convention rejected direct vote because of the concern that, due to the difficulty in getting information out, people would vote only for their "favorite sons."

The Electoral College was a compromise. It would allow voters to vote for electors who would then cast their votes for the candidates. The total number of a state's electors is equal to the number of senators, two, and the number of representatives, which is based on the state's population. On the Monday following the second Wednesday in December, the electors meet in their respective state capitals to cast their ballots for President and Vice President. The ballots are sealed and delivered to the president of the Senate. On January 6, in front of both houses of Congress, the ballots are opened and read.

Most of the time the electors cast their ballots for the candidate who received the most popular vote. There have been exceptions. Four presidents have been elected although they did not receive the most popular vote: John Quincy Adams, Rutherford B. Hayes, Benjamin Hayes, and George W. Bush.

Representatives, and Supreme Court would determine which of the contested votes to count. Originally, the commission was to have seven Republicans, seven Democrats, and one Independent. Before the commission actually met, though, the Independent, a Supreme Court justice, resigned and was replaced by a Republican.

The political division of the commission could be seen in the results of their decisions.

*A **filibuster** is an attempt to delay action in Congress by taking advantage of the Senate rules allowing unlimited debate.*

All the Republicans on the commission gave the votes to the Republicans, while the Democrats gave them to the Democrats. Each of the twenty disputed electoral votes went to the Republicans with an 8 to 7 decision.

The Democrats were outraged at the commission's decision. It was clear to them that the results were unfair, since there had been more Republicans than Democrats. The Democrats in the Senate protested, threatening a **filibuster** to keep the commission from officially reporting their decision.

A Centennial Celebration

The Centennial Exposition of 1876 in Philadelphia was a celebration of one hundred years of American independence and a display of new innovations in science and technology. Most of all, it was a celebration of progress. Nations from all over the world came to the Expo to display things unique to their own cultures, but a quarter of the displays belonged to the United States. The Expo was a chance for America to show the world that it truly had become a thriving, growing nation.

The Expo ran from January 1 to November 10. Manufacturers brought factory machines to demonstrate and newspapers such as the *New York Times* printed their daily editions in the Main Hall for spectators to watch.

The first telephone and the first typewriter were both on display, but of all the things to see people were most amazed by the Corliss Steam Engine. The engine towered over all the other displays and—to the amazement of visitors—powered all of the machines in the huge hall.

Time was running out; the new President was to be sworn in on March 4, 1877, and a winner had not yet been declared. Finally, the Democrats agreed to let Hayes take office as President in exchange for his agreement to take the rest of the federal troops out of the South. The agreement came to be known as the Compromise of 1877 and also included the promise of federal money to help build a southern railroad line. On March 2, 1877, Hayes was named as the winner of the 1876 election.

Before being elected President, Rutherford Hayes had enjoyed a reputation for being scrupulously honest. Despite the fact that Hayes was personally uninvolved with the scandal, the election of 1876 took its toll on Hayes's reputation. Democrats claimed that the election had been "stolen" from Tilden and sometimes bitterly referred to Hayes as "Rutherfraud."

President Hayes weathered the scandal and went on to work hard to end the corruption at all levels of government. Besides reducing political corruption, he also signed a bill during his presidency that allowed female attorneys to argue cases before the U.S. Supreme Court.

When the last federal troops left the South, Southern governments quickly came back to the control of the Democrats. The black population, which had been granted rights and freedoms during the Reconstruction years, found itself to some extent abandoned. The Democratic state governments, reestablished after the withdrawal of the federal troops, organized segregation, separating blacks from the white population and limiting their freedoms as much as the Constitution would allow.

The Civil War freed the black slaves and the Constitutional amendments of the Reconstruction granted the freedmen citizenship and gave voting rights to adult black males. With the end of Reconstruction, however, the country generally lost interest in the lives of Southern black people. They were no longer being enslaved, and this was enough to satisfy most of the nation. It would be nearly another hundred years before the Civil Rights movement and the end of legal segregation.

The Centennial Exposition in Philadelphia

1820 The Missouri Compromise is passed, agreeing not to admit any more slave states north of Missouri's southern border.

1619 A Dutch ship trades twenty Africans to the Jamestown colonists. These first Africans are treated as indentured servants.

1850 The Compromise of 1850. This series of laws is designed to satisfy both the North and the South. Included in the Compromise is the Fugitive Slave Act.

1850 California joins the Union as a free state, upsetting the balance between slave and free states.

1846–1848 Mexican War was fought over Texas.

1793 Eli Whitney patents the cotton gin.

May 1856 Senator Charles Sumner is attacked in the Senate Chamber by South Carolina Representative Preston Brooks two days after Sumner delivered a speech called "The Crime Against Kansas."

1861 The Southern states form the Confederate States of America. The Confederate Army fires shots at the Union-held Fort Sumter in South Carolina. The Union commander surrenders the fort to South Carolina. This is the first battle of the Civil War.

1860 Unhappy that Lincoln is elected President, South Carolina secedes from the Union followed by Mississippi, Florida, Alabama, Georgia, Louisiana, and Texas.

1858 Abraham Lincoln runs against Stephen Douglas in the Illinois Senate race. They argue the expansion of slavery; Lincoln against, Douglas for it. Douglas wins the election.

1856 Bushwhackers and Jayhawkers (proslavery advocates and abolitionists) fight for control of Kansas.

A Civil War reenenactment

September 22, 1862 Lincoln issues the Emancipation Proclamation. This changes the focus of the war from simply keeping the country together to ending slavery.

July 1–3, 1863 The Battle of Gettysburg is fought. The largest battle ever fought in the Western Hemisphere, it marks the turning point of the Civil War in favor of the North.

November 1863 President Lincoln delivers the Gettysburg Address at the dedication of the Soldiers' National Cemetery.

Autumn 1864 Union General William T. Sherman's March to the Sea, a destructive and effective campaign to take Georgia. Sherman reached Savannah in December and wrote to President Lincoln offering him the city as a Christmas gift.

1868 The House of Representatives impeaches President Andrew Johnson. They are unhappy with the way he has handled the reconstruction of the South. Johnson is acquitted in the Senate.

April 14, 1865 President Abraham Lincoln is shot by John Wilkes Booth while attending a performance at Ford's Theatre. He dies the next morning.

1876   The presidential election turns controversial when neither the Republican candidate, Rutherford B. Hayes, nor the Democratic candidate, Samuel J. Tilden, receives the required number of electoral votes. Twenty electoral votes are in dispute. A commission of eight Republicans and seven Democrats gives all the votes to Hayes.

April 9, 1865 Confederate General Robert E. Lee surrenders to Union General Ulysses S. Grant after the battle of Appomattox Courthouse. Lee's surrender ends the Civil War.

March 2, 1867 Congress passes the Reconstruction Act, disbanding Southern state governments and sending in Northern troops to govern the area.

Pickett's Charge during the battle at Gettysburg

FURTHER READING

Alter, Judy. *Andrew Johnson*. Berkeley Heights, N.J.: MyReportLinks.com, 2002.

Batty, Peter and Peter Parish. *The Divided Union: The Story of the Great American War, 1861–65*. Topsfield, Mass.: Salem House, 1987.

Bial, Raymond. *The Underground Railroad*. Boston: Houghton Mifflin, 1995.

Biel, Timothy Levi. *Life in the North During the Civil War*. San Diego: Lucent, 1997.

Bolotin, Norman. *Civil War: A to Z*. New York: Dutton Children's Books, 2002.

Brash, Sarah, ed. *War Between Brothers*. Alexandria, Va.: Time-Life, 1996.

Burchard, Peter. *Lincoln and Slavery*. New York: Atheneum, 1999.

Chang, Ina. *A Separate Battle: Women and the Civil War*. New York: Lodestar, 1991.

Clark, Champ. *The Assassination: Death of a President*. Alexandria, Va.: Time-Life, 1987.

Corrick, James A. *Life Among the Soldiers and Cavalry*. San Diego, Calif.: Lucent, 2000.

Damon, Duane. *Growing Up in the Civil War*. Minneapolis: Lerner, 2003.

Dubowski, Cathy East. *Robert E. Lee and the Rise of the South*. Englewood Cliffs, N.J.: Silver Burdett, 1991.

Fradin, Dennis Brindell. *Bound for the North Star: True Stories of Fugitive Slaves*. New York: Clarion, 2000.

Franklin, John Hope. *Reconstruction After the Civil War*. Chicago: University of Chicago Press, 1961.

Korn, Jerry. *Pursuit to Appomattox: The Last Battles*. Alexandria, Va.: Time-Life, 1987.

Lawson, Don. *The United States in the Civil War*. New York: Abelard-Schuman, 1977.

Levenson, Dorothy. *The First Book of the Confederacy*. New York: Franklin Watts, 1968.

Marrin, Albert. *Unconditional Surrender: U.S. Grant and the Civil War*. New York: Atheneum, 1994.

Metzger, Larry. *Abraham Lincoln*. New York: Franklin Watts, 1987.

Murphy, Richard W. *The Nation Reunited: War's Aftermath.* Alexandria, Va.: Time-Life, 1989.

O'Brien, Steven. *Ulysses S. Grant.* New York: Chelsea House, 1991.

Ray, Delia. *A Nation Torn: The Story of How the Civil War Began.* New York: Puffin, 1996.

Reef, Catherine. *Gettysburg.* New York: Dillon, 1992.

Shorto, Russell. *Abraham Lincoln and the End of Slavery.* Brookfield, Conn.: Millbrook, 1991.

Smith, Carter, ed. *One Nation Again.* Brookfield, Conn.: Millbrook, 1993.

Smith, Carter, ed. *Prelude to War.* Brookfield, Conn.: Millbrook, 1993.

Weidhorn, Manfred. *Robert E. Lee.* New York: Atheneum, 1988.

FOR MORE INFORMATION

Slavery
www.digitalhistory.uh.edu/black_voices/black_voices.cfm

A Civil War Timeline
www.historyplace.com/civilwar

The Civil War
www.swcivilwar.com
www.civilwar.com
americancivilwar.com

Abraham Lincoln
members.aol.com/RVSNorton/Lincoln2.html

Reconstruction
americanhistory.about.com/cs/reconstruction

BIOGRAPHIES

AUTHOR

Sheila Nelson has always been fascinated with history and the lives of historical figures. When she was twelve years old, she memorized Longfellow's poem, "Paul Revere's Ride," after she realized the event had taken place on her birthday. Later, she was able to study history more formally and enjoyed learning more about the events and people that have shaped our world. Sheila recently completed a master's degree and now lives in Rochester, New York, with her husband and their baby daughter. She has written several other titles in this series.

SERIES CONSULTANT

Dr. Jack N. Rakove is a professor of history and American studies at Stanford University, where he is director of American studies. The winner of the 1997 Pulitzer Prize in history, Dr. Rakove is the author of *The Unfinished Election of 2000, Constitutional Culture and Democratic Rule,* and *James Madison and the Creation of the American Republic.* He is also the president of the Society for the History of the Early American Republic.

PICTURE CREDITS

George N. Barnard, Dover: pp. 64–65
Mathew Brady, Dover: pp. 55, 72
CivilWarPhotos.net: pp. 13, 74–75
Corel: pp. 50–51
Currier & Ives: p. 77
Dover: pp. 36, 48, 56, 58–59, 70–71
Fort Caroline, Kingsley Plantation: pp. 8–9, 10, 11
Alexander Gardner, Dover: p. 39
Gettysburg Convention and Visitors Bureau: pp. 35, 63, 80–81, 86–87
John Grafton, Dover: pp. 42–43, 45, 46–47, 49
Library of Congress: pp. 36–37, 41, 60–61, 68
Museum of Philadelphia: pp. 84–85
National Archives and Records Administration: pp. 12, 17, 24, 29, 33, 53, 66–67, 69
PhotoDisc: pp. 88–89
Photos.com: cover, pp. 12, 13, 15, 53, 54, 57, 96
Benjamin Stewart, Fort Caroline, Kingsley Plantation: pp. 11, 28
Benjamin Stewart: pp. 18–19, 20
Studio Series International One: p. 82
University of Illinois at Chicago: p. 18
U. S. Senate: p. 78
WildsidePress: p. 38
White House: p. 44
Yale University: p. 11